TEXAS HIGHWAY HUMOR

Wallace O. Chariton

Wordware Publishing, Inc.
 REGIONAL DIVISION

Library of Congress Cataloging-in-Publication Data

Chariton, Wallace O.
    Texas highway humor / Wallace O. Chariton.
        p.   cm.
    ISBN 1-55622-176-2
    1. Texas—Description and travel—Humor   2. American wit and
humor—Texas.   I. Title.
F386.6.C47   1991
976.4'00207—dc20   90-26498
                                                               CIP

Copyright © 1992, Wordware Publishing, Inc.

1506 Capital Avenue
Plano, Texas 75074

Printed in the United States of America

ISBN 1-55622-176-2

10 9 8 7 6 5 4 3 2 1

9109

All inquiries for volume purchases of this book should be addressed to
Wordware Publishing, Inc., at the above address. Telephone inquiries
may be made by calling:
(214) 423-0090

Contents

Dedication

This one is for Dave Williams. He knows why.

Acknowledgements

A big Texas thanks to: Diane Bruce; Judge Bob Hefner; R. V. Miller, Jr.; Glenn Raines, Jr.; Roy Lee Smith; the late Bernice Strong; Don Weigand; a certain highway patrolman from the Texas Department of Public Safety who preferred to remain nameless; Doug Miller of Perfection Paint & Body, Inc. in Lewisville, Texas, for allowing me to use photographs of his display for the front and back covers; and finally to all the advertising folks and other creative people who are responsible for humor along the Texas highways.

Preface

I first started traveling the highways of Texas in the back seat of my parents' old Mercury in the early 1950s. Four decades later, I'm still traveling in a Mercury only now I have to do most of the driving.

As a kid, the trips were often long and boring. It seemed to take an eternity to go from Fort Worth to San Antonio. It did take an eternity to go from San Antonio to Muleshoe. Without any brothers or sisters to fight with, there wasn't much to do but sleep and ask when we'd get there. I can still remember my mother trying to defuse my boredom by encouraging me to watch for the Burma Shave signs. It always worked, at least for a little while.

In the late 1920s, the Burma Shave company was trying to get men to change to shaving lather from a jar rather than using the old brush-and-mug method that had been around for generations. To encourage men to make the switch, the company conceived a plan that would make advertising history. They painted lines from clever verses on wooden signs and then put them up along the side of roads all over the nation, including Texas.

The signs were an instant hit. Laughing at the simple verses seemed to break the monotony of long drives. Unexpectedly perhaps, the signs also provided the added bonus of giving parents a tool to keep children occupied. Some families, mine included, would use the Burma Shave signs as an inspiration to create our own verses. It was great fun and making up verses always seemed to make time pass quicker.

The Burma Shave sign program ended in the early sixties and today, the few remaining signs are prized collectors' items. Although the signs are gone, they are not forgotten. Here's some samples of the famous verses, all of which appeared in Texas:

**Little Bo-Peep • Has Lost Her Jeep • It Struck A
Truck • When She Went To Sleep • Burma Shave**

Remember This • If You'd Be Spared • Trains Don't
Whistle • Because They're Scared • Burma Shave

Cover • A Multitude • Of Chins • Pays Dividends •
In Lady Friends • Burma Shave

Shaving Brush • Was Like • Old Rover •
When He Died • He Died • All Over • Burma Shave

Bachelor's Quarters • Dog On The Rug • Whiskers
To Blame • No One • To Hug • Burma Shave

Baby Your Skin • Keep It Fitter • Or "Baby" •
Will Get • Another Sitter • Burma Shave

'Twould Be • More Fun • To Go By Air • If We
Could Put • These Signs Up There • Burma Shave

Approached • A Crossing • Without Looking •
Who Will Eat • His Widow's Cooking • Burma Shave

Brother Speeders • Let's • Rehearse • All Together •
"Good Morning, Nurse!" • Burma Shave

Cattle Crossing • Means Go Slow • That Old
Bull • Is Some • Cow's Beau • Burma Shave

Don't Lose • Your Head • To Gain A Minute • You Need
Your Head • Your Brains Are In It • Burma Shave

If You • Must Sample • Her "Pucker Paint" • Better
Drive • Where Traffic Ain't • Burma Shave

At Intersections • Look Each Way • A Harp Sounds
Nice • But It's Hard To Play • Burma Shave

Noah Had Whiskers • In The Ark • But He Wouldn't
Get By • On A Bench • In The Park • Burma Shave

Since the Burma Shave signs inspired my interest in Texas
highway humor, you'll find more of the classic verses scattered
throughout this book. You'll also find a lot of other humor that was
seen, at one time or another, somewhere in Texas. I hope you have
as much fun with this book as I did in bringing it to you.

Wallace O. Chariton

Photo Credits

Abbreviations used to identify picture sources are:
BC - Barker Texas History Center, Austin
DA - Duplex Advertising Company, Temple
DRT - Daughters of the Republic of Texas Library at the Alamo
DTH - Dallas/Texas History Collection, Dallas Public Library
GL - Glenn Raines, Jr., Rockwall
HPL - Houston Public Library
ITC - Institute of Texan Cultures, San Antonio
KBVO Television, Austin
MLE - Mary Lou Edwards, Austin
OASS - Outdoor Advertising Sales & Service
RS - Roy Smith, Eastland
SA - Texas State Archives, Austin

Position are Top - T; Middle - M; Bottom - B. All photographs not listed are from the author's collection.
3T - DRT; 3B - DTH; 4B - ITC; 5T&B - DRT; 6T - DRT; 7T - DRT; 7B - RS; 8B - DRT; 9T - DTH; 9B - ITC; 14 - ITC; 22 T&B - RS; 23T&B - RS; 26T&B - DTH; 27T&B - DTH; 28B - DTH; 29T - ITC; 29B - DTH; 30T - DTH; 31T - DTH; 35T&B - RS; 37T&B - HPL; 38T - HPL; 38B - GL; 39T - ITC; 40T&B - DTH; 41T&B - DTH; 44T - ITC; 45T - ITC; 45B - DTH; 46 - ITC; 48 - ITC; 49T - DTH; 50B - ITC; 51 - ITC; 54T - ITC; 55T - ITC; 55B - DTH; 56T - DTH; 56B - ITC; 57T - DRT; 57B - DTH; 58T - DTH; 59T - MLE; 60T - RS; 60B - DTH; 61T - ITC; 61B - DTH; 62B - KBVO; 63T&B - DTH; 64T&B - DTH; 65T - ITC; 65B - DTH; 66T - ITC; 66B - DTH; 67T&B - DTH; 69T&B - DTH; 70T - ITC; 70B - DRT; 71T - ITC; 71B - DTH; 72T&B- DTH; 73T - DTH; 5B 78T - DTH; 78B - ITC; 79T - DTH; 91T - DTH; 91B - DRT; 92T - DRT; 92B - DTH; 93B - ITC; 121 - ITC; 122T&B - DTH; 123 - 127 - DA; 134B - OASS; 135T - OASS; 137 - OASS; 138T - OASS

PART ONE

Revolution

In the beginning
it was . . .

. . . Happy Trails

There has always been a special bond between Texans and their horses. The fact is, if it wasn't for horses, there might not even be a Texas. Spaniards came here on horseback and a lot of the animals stayed behind when the explorers went home. When Americans ventured into Texas, they either came on a horse or quickly caught and broke one of the leftover Spanish ponies. The Mexican cavalry came on horses when they grew tired of having Americans in their Texas. The best light cavalry in the world — the American Indian — used horses in a vain attempt to stall the advance of the white man into Texas. And the Indians might have won if the U.S. Army hadn't had more men and more horses! When there wasn't fighting to be done, Texas cowboys were using horses to herd the longhorns and Texas farmers were using mules to tame the land. When the work was done, there were even more possibilities.

A person could put on his best Sunday clothes and go for a ride in the country or . . .

. . . hitch a horse to a buggy and go courtin' with a favorite companion.

If a buggy wasn't handy, couples could "get together" and go for a ride on a horse. Or . . .

. . . the family could saddle up some burros and head off to see sights like the famous balanced rock. Of course, burros were occasionally in short supply and someone had to walk. One reason burros were often scarce is that some of them were . . .

. . . hitched to the family station wagon. The scarceness of burros may have lead to the invention of the world's first . . .

. . . 4 X 4 (as in four hooves by four hooves).

There seems little doubt that life was so much simpler back then, but there were still some problems that had to be faced.

Occasionally, riders weren't exactly matched to their mounts or . . .

. . . the animals weren't exactly matched with each other.

There were frequent unexpected fuel stops and . . .

. . . the occasional road turned into a swamp.

There were also problems like broken wheels . . .

. . . and blown oxen. Sadly, oxen almost never came with a 50,000-mile road hazard warranty.

Even if the equipment worked properly you still had to be wary of the . . .

8

... police cruiser and the ...

... highway patrol!

Despite the problems and frequent inconveniences, the love affair between Texans and their horses continued unabated. As late as 1890, there were twice as many horses in Texas as there were people. It has been said that most of the early Texans learned to ride a horse before they could walk.

Although the horses never knew it, they were an essential part of the economy of Texas. Every town in the state had to have a blacksmith to keep the trotters and steppers in form-fitted iron shoes. There had to be a livery stable to provide accommodations for the animals, which included feed from the local general store or hay from a local farmer.

To get the most out of the horse, there had to be saddles, blankets, bridles, reins, brushes, morel bags, spurs and the like, all of which had to come from somewhere, usually the local general store. For people with plenty to carry, there were wagon and buggy companies happy to supply the vehicles. People who didn't actually own a horse could travel in a horse-drawn stagecoach. In addition to people, stagecoaches also carried the mail and some freight. Yes, life was a lot simpler — so much so that even pollution caused by horses could be cleaned up with a shovel and recycled in the garden.

By the early 1890s, however, the winds of change were beginning to stir. Texans heard of and marveled at such inventions as electricity and the telephone, but few could imagine that just around the technological corner lurked a dastardly invention called the . . .

. . . horseless carriage.

Although some will argue, credit for inventing the carriage without a horse usually goes to Charles and Frank Duryea of Massachusetts. The brothers, like perhaps hundreds of others, spent some time tinkering around in their garage trying to build a carriage that would run without a horse. In 1893 the Duryea boys succeeded when they produced their first Motor Wagon (previous page).

Most Texans didn't think the horseless carriage had much merit. After all, trusty horses had helped the people of Texas transform a wilderness into a decent place to live and work. Not one Texan in a thousand would have believed it if you had proclaimed that the introduction of the horseless carriage meant that the days of the horse being king of the Texas road were numbered. They wouldn't have believed you but then most Texans had never heard of a bankrupt tractor maker named Henry Ford.

While the Duryea brothers busied themselves with establishing a company to market the new "toys," inventors around the world continued to experiment and tinker around with carriages and motors. One inventor, George Selden, was successful enough that he applied for and received a U.S. patent on his two-cylinder automobile in 1895.

Perhaps the most dramatic development in early automobile history came in 1896 when the very first . . .

. . . Ford Automobile was introduced.

11

Although Ford had failed in his effort to replace the mule-drawn plow with a mechanized steam-driven tractor, he had, inadvertently, set the stage for unseating the horse as the king of the prairie. But the unseating would not be a simple proposition in Texas.

The first public display of a horseless carriage in Texas was on April 20, 1897, when a special train from Montgomery Ward & Co. pulled into Dallas. The train carried a mobile display of the company's latest offerings, one of which was a carriage powered by a small electric motor in place of a horse. The carriage was carefully unloaded and many interested, although skeptical, spectators were given free rides around the courthouse in an attempt to spur interest and sales. It was a nice try on the part of Montgomery Ward but the company didn't win any cigars. Not a single Texan, most of whom still believed in the horse, placed an order that day and, as it turned out, it would be two years before any Texan would actually own an automobile.

The honor for being the first person in Texas to actually own a horseless carriage goes to the Honorable E. H. R. Green of Terrell, Texas. Green, son of eccentric stock dealer Hettie Green (better known as "the Witch of Wall Street"), was chairman of the State Republican Executive Committee on October 3, 1899 when he took delivery of a two-cylinder, five-horsepower St. Louis automobile. Unfortunately, no one thought to take a picture of the momentous event.

For two days Green puttered around Terrell, but then on October 5, 1899, he decided to make history. He enlisted the aid of a local automobile expert (although how there could have been any local experts since Green's was the first car in Texas has never been explained) and set off for Dallas, more than thirty miles to the west. The trip, which began about 2:30 in the afternoon, was quite an adventure.

Near Forney, Green's automobile was forced off the road and into a gully by a horse-drawn farm wagon. The accident caused damage to the water tank on the St. Louis which necessitated a stop at a blacksmith shop for repairs. That event surely qualifies as the first automobile accident and the first repair job in Texas history. Once the tank was mended, Green and his mysterious co-pilot continued their journey. After a five-hour trip, during which two quarts of gasoline were consumed, the adventurers reached Dallas about 7:30 pm. Green drove up and down Main

Street, at speeds estimated to be fifteen miles per hour. Naturally, the press turned out to hear Green's description of the trip.

"When we left Terrell," Green said to a *Dallas Morning News* reporter, "we struck a very sandy stretch of road, and because of the dust thrown up by the vehicle, we had to go very slowly. After this bad stretch was passed we turned on more power and fairly flew."

"It was interesting to notice the sensation our appearance caused along the road," Green continued. "Cotton pickers dropped their sacks and ran wildly to the fence to see the strange sight. And the interest was shared by the farm animals, too. One razor-back sow that caught sight of us is running still, I know. At least a dozen horses executed fancy waltz steps on their hind legs as we sped swiftly by, and but for the fact that we went so soon out of sight, there would have been several first-class runaways. When we reached Dallas, however, the city horses, used to electric streetcars and other things alarming to most equines, did not even lift their heads."

"I have no idea of the speed of the vehicle," he continued. "We did not put on full power on the country roads because it would have been too dusty for comfort, and when we struck the asphalt pavement on Main Street we dared not do so because the thoroughfare was so crowded it would have been dangerous to human life. I enjoyed my trip immensely and intend to make many more like it in the near future."

THE PASSING OF THE HORSE

This cartoon illustrated what usually happened when an automobile and horse-drawn wagon met on the trail.

Green did make more trips — many more. But there were some major problems. It seems some of the farmers in the Terrell area noticed that their cows suddenly stopped giving milk. The farmers blamed the automobile and Green ended up in court defending his machine.

Although the appearance of Green's St. Louis may have started the ball rolling for the automobile industry in Texas, the ball did not roll fast. Texans continued to cling to the notion that automobiles were little more than toys that had practically no commercial value. As surprising as it might seem today, one reason for that skepticism was a lack of oil.

The situation began to change on the morning of January 10, 1901, near a place called Spindletop Bayou in southwestern Liberty County, Texas. A. F. Lucas, drilling in a salt dome where the experts had said there was no oil, brought in one of the largest producing wells in history. The well came in flowing an amazing 75,000 barrels of oil a day which was a quantity unheard of in the entire world. The great Lucas gusher was destined to change the world because that one well has been credited with ushering in the liquid fuel age. Suddenly, it seemed, gasoline was in plentiful supply and the whole world had Texas to thank.

By 1903 the automobile revolution was beginning to take shape, thanks in large part to ol' Henry Ford. That year Henry introduced his sleek new . . .

. . . one-cylinder Fordmobile and many of the cars, like the one above, were purchased by Texans. Despite many skeptics, Henry showed 'em all. The 1903 model was an instant success and Ford was on his way to automobile immortality.

Even though the automobile was becoming a reality in Texas by 1903, there was still some room for doubt about the viability of the machines. A lot of people still considered the vehicles as merely "toys." In fact, a special column in the *Dallas Morning News* was labeled, in 1903, as "The Automobile Fad." The "Fad" column for August 23, 1903, contained a recap of what was going on in Dallas concerning automobiles:

"Dallas, it is now said, enjoys the distinction of possessing more automobiles than any city of its size in the south. This assertion is based upon the fact that there are owned in Dallas at this time over forty autos, besides those carried by dealers in stock, and six others are on the way, while the dealers say that there is not a week that passes in which at least one automobile is not sold.

"Radiating out from Dallas there are many roads which are suited to automobiling and every fair afternoon of the week can be seen the spectacle of many autos streaking out of the city. These roads, it is stated, are reasonably good within a radius of twenty-five miles of Dallas, and that the greater number of these roads are made within that distance, particularly because there is no means of storing electricity in the electric machines this side of Fort Worth after they leave Dallas, and the power contained in the average electric machine will not permit a longer trip.

"But Dallas is rich in gasoline machines and in steamery, and a number of long journeys have been taken — long considering the type and size of the vehicles owned here. There are no very large machines here, most of them being of the runabout type and generally considered unsuited for tours.

"The largest at the time is a four-passenger, ten-horsepower car but most are two-passenger, five-horse versions.

"The auto drivers are in the habit of assembling at 375 Main Street and starting off in bunches, particularly on Sunday afternoons. They take a swift drive of a few miles and return, cool and refreshed. And when they return there is no sweating horse to rub down, no dusty harness to remove and hang up.

"There is considerable talk at present of an auto club, formed by those who own machines, and it is stated that this must come sooner or later, and will probably come sooner.

"One thing in favor of a club being formed lies in the fact that the proposition to have auto races at the state fair has been seized upon by the auto possessors as one of the most promising prospects extant. There may be professionals with the genuine man-killing juggernauts of which everyone has read — great machines as big as locomotives that can make a mile a minute without half trying.

"They point with pride to the great number of autos in Dallas and say it would be a shame to have auto races of this sort and no club to back them up. They also point with pride to the ascending market quotations on gasoline, saying that in Dallas you can not get gasoline now for less than .85, sometimes .96, whereas a short time ago it was quoted at .65, and auger from this that Dallas is swiftly reaching a point where it will be known at home and abroad as a city of automobiles."

Exactly why it was good news that gasoline prices had risen from 65 cents to 85 cents or more per gallon is not clear, but the spirit of the story was simply that Dallas had arrived as an automobile city. And Big D wasn't the only Texas city getting in on the fad.

In May 1903 the Fort Worth city council became so concerned about the proliferation of motorized vehicles that they passed ordinances regulating the use of automobiles. The ordinances required that each automobile be registered with the city secretary, and that the license number assigned be painted on the body in numbers at least six inches high. The speed limit was set at 10 miles per hour within the Fort Worth city limits. Each vehicle was required to have two headlights that could be seen for a quarter of a mile at night and a horn or bell that could be heard a distance of 200 yards. Unfortunately, the council also declared that drivers were to begin sounding their horn 100 feet before reaching an intersection and continue sounding it until the street had been crossed. If the prediction about the popularity of automobiles was to come true, Fort Worth was going to be a noisy place.

In Houston, where there was said to be several dozen automobiles by 1903, city officials feared that the machines might soon become so numerous that "pedestrians will be constantly endangered and the automobiles themselves may frequently collide." As a result of that fear, the officials passed regulations concerning the proper use of the new toys. The Houston ordinances resulted in a first for Texas when an automobile driver was arrested and sent to jail for exceeding the speed limit of six miles per hour. He was later released after paying a $10 fine.

Beginning in 1903, the automobile slowly started to shed the "fad" label. It was becoming increasingly clear that automobiles were here to stay. No one knew that more than Henry Ford. He embarked on a spirited campaign to take his affordable automobiles to the people. But there was a problem. George B. Selden had a patent, issued on November 5, 1895, granting him the right to produce gasoline motor cars. Selden, in turn, licensed selected manufactures, including Packard, Olds, and Cadillac, to produce automobiles and pay him royalties. It might have been the sweetest deal in history except for Henry Ford.

Ford did not think the patent was legal and decided to go to court rather than pay royalties. In a sense, the automobile war was on. The Association of Licensed Automobile Manufacturers began an advertisement campaign to announce that they — and only they — could produce gasoline powered automobiles. Their advertisements proclaimed:

"No other manufacturers or importers are authorized to make or sell gasoline automobiles, and any person making, selling or using such machines made or sold by any unlicensed manufacturers or importers will be liable to prosecution for infringement."

In essence, the A.L.A.M. was advising people "not to buy a lawsuit when they bought a car." Ford countered with its own campaign, frequently running advertisements next to the A.L.A.M. group. Ford's ad, addressed to dealers, importers, agents, and users of gasoline automobiles proclaimed:

"We will protect you against any prosecution from alleged infringements of patents . . . the Selden patent is not a broad one, and if it was, it is anticipated. It does not cover a practical machine, no practical machine can be made from it and never was so far as we can ascertain . . . No court in the United States has ever decided in favor of the patent on the merits of the case . . . ."

**He Married Grace · With Scratchy Face · He Only ·
Got One Day · Of Grace · Burma Shave**

17

This Ford ad, which appeared in many publications that were distributed in Texas during 1904, not only told of the new eight-horsepower, two-cylinder engine, but also assured Texans that Ford would assume all responsibility for any suit of patent infringement.

The patent fight raged on but Ford kept selling automobiles all over the nation, including Texas. In 1909 the court ruled against Ford, but the decision was reversed in 1911 when the court decided the Selden patent was only for automobiles using the long-outmoded Brayton-type, two-cycle engine. Everyone, Ford included, was free to make gasoline automobiles.

By 1907 the horseless carriage label had almost vanished and the automobile was becoming more and more a part of everyday life in Texas. With the popularity, however, came some chaos. Almost every city scrambled to formulate its own policies and ordinances governing the use of motorized vehicles. For the traveler, whose range was beginning to extend far beyond the 20 or 25 miles of just a few years earlier, it became increasingly difficult to know what the rules were for a particular place they might be passing. Finally, on April 15, 1907, the state of Texas, after receiving repeated requests for action, passed the first official Texas laws regulating automobiles. The high points of the original law were as follows:

SECTION 1. All owners of automobiles or motor vehicles shall, before using such vehicles upon the public roads, register with the county clerk his name which shall be registered by the clerk in consecutive order in a book, and shall be numbered in the order of their registration, and it shall be the duty of such owner to display the number so registered in figures not less than six inches in height. The county clerk shall be paid a fee of fifty cents for each machine registered.

SEC. 2. No automobile or motor vehicle shall be operated at a greater rate of speed than eighteen miles an hour, or upon any public road within the built up portions of any city, town or village at a greater rate of speed than eighteen miles per hour, except where ordinance or by-laws allow a greater rate of speed, provided the speed limit shall not apply to race courses or speedways.

SEC. 3. No person in charge of an automobile shall drive the same at any speed greater than is reasonable and proper or so as to endanger the life or limb of any person thereon.

SEC. 4. All drivers or operators of automobiles or motor vehicles are prohibited from racing upon any public road, street or driveway.

SEC. 5. Any person driving or operating an automobile shall at the request, or signal by putting up the hand, or by other visible signal from a person riding or driving a horse or horses or other domestic animal, cause such machine to come to a standstill as quickly as possible and to remain stationary long enough to allow such animal to pass.

SEC. 6. Every driver or operator of an automobile shall have attached thereto a suitable bell for giving notice of its approach, so that when rung it may be heard a distance of three hundred feet, and shall carry a lighted lamp between one hour after [sundown] and one hour before sunrise.

SEC. 7. Every one who violates any of these six sections shall be punished by a fine of not less than five dollars nor more than one hundred dollars.

The laws were a sure sign that automobiles were gaining respectability. Despite the fact that drivers of motorized vehicles still had to yield to anyone operating a horse-drawn rig, it was clear that the automobile had arrived. But even so, some of the old doubts lingered.

As late as 1905 an editor of a Bonham, Texas, newspaper predicted, "Automobiles will never become as popular as buggies have been with young people. A man may drive with one hand and entertain his female companion with the other. He cannot manage an automobile with one hand and make his companion happy at the same time." In Houston, a man wrote that he wouldn't be in the market for a horseless carriage until "they start burning hay instead of gasoline." In San Antonio, another Texan proclaimed he wouldn't think of spending money on a vehicle that "couldn't find its own way home after he'd been out celebrating."

Most pessimists predicted automobiles would not catch on because they scared horses. There is evidence that three companies — one in Texas — attempted to market wooden horse heads that could be mounted on the front of automobiles. The theory, apparently, was that horses wouldn't be so scared if the automobiles looked a little like real horses. Another Texas company tried to market special "saddle seats" for automobiles so cowboys would be more at home behind the wheel. Neither idea worked.

Although some doubters still remained, by 1907 the automobile revolution was all but over and automobile evolution was already under way.

Part Two

Evolution

The automobile brought many
changes to Texas. Some of the
first things to change were the
streets. The changes were
necessary because if there was
one thing Texas had plenty of
it was ...

. . . mud, . . .

. . . lots and lots of mud!

**Romances Are Wrecked • Before They Begin • By A Hair •
On The Coat • Or A Lot On The Chin • Burma Shave**

Some people accepted the situation when they got stuck and went fishing while waiting for help to arrive. Others . . .

. . . found profit in mud by using horses to haul stranded motorists out of the quagmire for a price.

**The Whale • Put Jonah • Down The Hatch • But Coughed
Him Up • Because He Scratched • Burma Shave**

Mud presented a formidable obstacle to the advancement of the automobile in Texas. Early cars had large, thin tires that were reasonably effective in loose dirt and even in deep sand. But when the rains came — and in parts of Texas they came often — the motoring public was generally brought to a boggy halt. While the muddy roads were a severe drawback to automobiling, some people saw mud as a source of profit. Whenever oil was discovered and a new boom town sprang up, entrepreneurs often created land ferries to haul oil speculators across the street for a fee that ranged from ten cents to ten dollars, depending on how bad the passenger wanted to get to the other side of the street.

The most enterprising mud operation was the farmer who had some strong plow mules. When water turned the crude roads into an impassable nightmare, the farmers always seemed to materialize with mules and ropes. The cost for a friendly tow usually ranged from one to ten dollars and up.

Some dishonest farmers did not wait for the rains to come. They would fill barrels from a handy well and just happen to spill them in some low spot in the road. A few well-placed barrels of water could create more mud than a monsoon. Unsuspecting motorists would be out for a tour on a sunny day when the roads were dry and then suddenly find themselves axle deep in a man-made mud hole. Before the car settled in the mire, the farmer would appear and offer to pull the car free for a price. A few artificial mud holes actually became legendary, such as one that was about halfway between Dallas and Rockwall in a low spot in the road. Some people claim the farmer who operated that particular mud operation earned enough money in six months to purchase a brand new Ford.

There were, of course, many possible solutions to the mud problem. Some cities, like Houston and Galveston, experimented with paving their streets with a mixture of gravel and crushed sea shells. That didn't work. Another idea was to pave the streets with bricks made of bois d'arc wood soaked in creosote. The wooden bricks were sturdy but whenever it rained, the surface became so slick the roads might as well have been paved with glass. The water also caused the bricks to swell and buckle, which gave motorists a rather bumpy ride.

The search for a solution continued. When Charles Lindberg made his historic solo flight across the Atlantic in 1927, some people immediately suggested that Lindberg and Henry Ford should join forces and create the "flying car," as depicted in the cartoon below, which could solve the problem by flying over the muddy roads. Ford and Lindberg never got together, and the flying car wasn't the answer because . . .

**If Daisies • Are Your • Favorite Flower • Keep Pushin'
Up Those • Miles-Per-Hour • Burma Shave**

. . . it didn't arrive in Texas until the mid-1950s when mud was no longer a problem.

The car portion proved it could handle the streets of Dallas.

**Men • With Whiskers • 'Neath Their Noses • Oughta
Have To Kiss • Like Eskimoses • Burma Shave**

As a car, the carplane could do one thing no airplane could manage — use the covered parking garage at the Adolphus Hotel in Dallas.

By the time the carplane finally appeared, mud wasn't such a big problem. In cities, mud was first conquered by bricks which became so popular that when new paving projects were launched, crowds often showed up for the . . .

. . . ceremonial placing of the first brick.

**If *HER* Whiskers • Scratched *YOUR* Cheek • You Would •
Send Her Out • To Seek • Burma Shave**

Unfortunately, bricks were not practical for long country roads. An alternative for rural areas was a crude, narrow concrete road. Some people were so proud of the early concrete highways that they would just stop, sit down on their car, and have their picture made for the folks back home. Unfortunately, those concrete roads were usually only wide enough for one car at a time, which means the game of automobile chicken may very well have been invented when motorists met going in opposite directions.

The rural situation was finally resolved by use of an oil-based, tar-like substance commonly called blacktop which is still used today throughout Texas.

If You Want • A Hearty Squeeze • Get • Our •
Female Anti-freeze • Burma Shave

Bridges were another problem for pioneer motorists. A lot of early bridges were extremely dangerous, especially if the driver turned his head to smile for the camera!

Concrete and steel ultimately replaced the wood but there was another problem: how to keep drivers in their lanes? The answer was to paint lane stripes on the bridge. Unfortunately, as shown above, the early stripes weren't very straight and drivers weren't very adept at staying between the lines.

Eventually, the solid lines became dashed lines. As to the problem of keeping things straight . . .

... that was solved by having someone walk beside the painter and offer instructions. The dashed white line has become commonplace but evolution may still be at work.

PAVEMENT MARKING TEST STRIPES AHEAD

In Fort Worth, someone is experimenting with a new striping method. Instead of the normal stripe pattern of dash-space-dash that has worked for generations, they are trying a new system of dash-dash-space dash-dash.

My question is, even if the new system were better, how much would it cost to change all the roads in Texas?

Today, we have modern super highways like the infamous Central Expressway in Dallas. This picture was taken shortly after the expressway opened in the mid-1950s and about two hours before it became obsolete.

The Dallas folks have tried everything to make Central less congested, including using special traffic lights at on-ramps. The lights are supposed to regulate traffic flow during peak hours. Fat chance! The only drivers who pay attention to these lights are tourists and the weak of heart.

Now, a new solution is being tried — the reconstruction of North Central Expressway, which began in 1990. A good bet is an estimated completion date somewhere in the 21st century would be a lot more accurate than any time in 1993.

Don't Lose • Your Head • To Gain A Minute • You Need
Your Head • Your Brains Are In It • Burma Shave

While the roads were evolving into something that made travel a little easier, the automobile makers were busy with their own evolutionary chores. None was more active, and more successful, than Henry Ford. In 1908 Ford introduced his . . .

. . . famous Model T. The cars were produced in various forms and styles for 19 years. And while some claim other automobiles were better, no one can deny that Ford sold more Model Ts to more people than any other car maker. Texans, like most other people, took to the Model T in huge numbers. And somewhere along the way, a unique love-hate relationship developed that became legendary. While people continued to drive their Model Ts, new names appeared for the unsinkable car such as: Bouncing Betty, Tin Lizzie, Leaping Leana, Galloping Snail, Flivver, and Spirit of St. Vitus. Some enterprising owners actually painted slogans on their Ts such as: Four Wheels, No Brakes; I Do Not Choose to Run; Beware - Old Faithful Spouts Every Five Minutes; FORD, Fix Or Repair Daily; and one that was popular among Texas farmers: Chicken, Here's Your Roost, implying the local chickens were about due for a new home.

His Crop Of • Whiskers • Needed Reaping • That's
What Kept • His Leana Leaping • Burma Shave

Naturally, the Model T provided inspiration for the newspaper cartoonist. Here's an example that appeared in the early 1920s under the headline "Evolution:"

Even though people made jokes about Ford's Model T, they continued to buy them in record numbers. But Henry Ford was not without competition. Eventually, more than 2,000 makes of automobiles were either manufactured in the United States or imported from foreign countries. While some survived, . . .

In Texas Oil Fields
"Where the goin' is rough"
The
TEXAN

—now entering its third year of making good, has established itself as a car—sturdy and dependable.

1920

Its mechanical units are of known quality and the coach work unexcelled.

Note the partial list of specifications appearing on this page. They are of known merit and in keeping with every other detail of construction in the Texan.

Partial Specifications.

Lycoming (4 Cylinder) Motor.
Borg & Beck Clutch.
Grant Lees Transmission.
Timken Bearings.
Detroit Universal Joint.
Boyce MotoMeter.
Custom Made Upholstering and Top.
Over Sized Tires (33x4) with 7,500 mile guarantee—regular equipment.
Wheel Base, 115 inches.
Road Weight, 2625 pounds.

Completion of additional units of our factory enables us, through increased production, to take on a few additional dealers. Write or wire us for full particulars.

Texas Motor Car Association
Fort Worth, Texas

Export Office, 28 Burling Slip
New York City

• • • POWER-HOUR AFTER HOUR • • •

... most did not and one of the casualties was the Texan, which was billed as being well-suited for Texas oil fields "where the goin' is rough." Regardless of the merits of the car, the slogan was correct because ...

... the goin' certainly was rough ...

... in the early Texas oil fields.

**Cautious Rider • To Her • Reckless Dear • Let's Have
Less Bull • And Lots More Steer • Burma Shave**

Competition among the automobile companies created many new marketing innovations, but none was more entertaining than the battle of the slogans. The manufacturers competed vigorously to find just the catch phrase that would entice the buyer to take the plunge. Here are some of the more famous early automobile catch phrases used to try to persuade Texans to buy:

American - Miles of smiles
Anderson - It's as roomy for five as it's chummy for two
Austin - A car to run around in
Bates - Buy a Bates and keep your dates
Cartermobile - The Wonder Car
Crestmobile - Better than any other at anywhere near the price
Dragon - The motor that motes
Durant - Just a real good car
Firestone Columbus - A mechanical greyhound
Gale - Climbs hills like a squirrel
Gearless - No tender or delicate parts
Glide - Ride in a Glide, then decide
Jackson - No hill too steep, no sand too deep
King - The car of no regrets
Knox - The car that obviates the tow
Marathon - Cars built for the long, hard run
Martin - The little brother of the aeroplane
Maxwell - Perfectly simple - simply perfect
Maytag - The hill climber
Metz - No clutch to slip, no gears to strip
Northern - Silent and dustless
Northern - Silent as the stars
Oakland - The car with a conscience
Owen-Magnetic - The car with a thousand speeds
Porter - The only perfect automobile
Roamer - America's smartest car
Sampson - Strong as its name suggests
Saxon - The car that makes both ends meet
Stoddard-Dayton - None can go farther, none can go faster
Studebaker - The automobile with a reputation behind it
Thomas - The car that shuns the repair shop
Union - In Union there is strength
Walter - The car of a hundred reasons

And my favorite: Nash - It's as catching as measles

As automobiles grew in popularity, another phase of evolution occurred when the . . .

. . . automobile dealership appeared. In the early days, before it was certain the automobile would take over, some dealers hedged their bet and sold buggies as well as automobiles.

The buggies gradually disappeared and the evolution of the automobile dealership continued.

Delux • De Looks • With Burma Shave

The dealership buildings became much larger . . .

. . . and eventually much more modern in design.

Cheek To Cheek · They Meant To Be · The Lights
Went Out · And So Did He · Burma Shave

Almost from the beginning, dealerships have tried to attract customers with special displays. This early example showed how a pickup could be used in place of the horse on hunting trips.

This modern display, in front of Sun Chevy in Dallas, was constructed in response to a TV advertisement showing a Ford pickup carrying a Chevy up a hill.

**Say, Big Boy • To Go • Thru Life • How'd You
Like • A Wiskered Wife? • Burma Shave**

When dealers weren't competing with displays, they tried to lure customers with the promise of fast, efficient, and reliable repair service using state-of-the-art machines and . . .

. . . efficient wreckers that could be sent out when you needed help, like when your engine ended up in the front seat.

**At Crossroads • Don't Just • Trust To Luck • The
Other Car • May Be A Truck • Burma Shave**

It wasn't long before the official service vehicle was born . . .

. . . and the mobile repair service truck wasn't far behind.

Another method the dealers used to convince customers to buy their brand was the special promotion. Before there was any such thing as "cash back" or "first time buyer's allowance" or "special option packages" there was some real creativity.

Saves The Jack • Holds Your Jill • Burma Shave

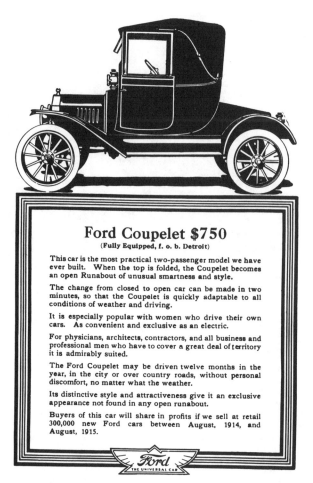

Ford Coupelet $750
(Fully Equipped, f. o. b. Detroit)

This car is the most practical two-passenger model we have ever built. When the top is folded, the Coupelet becomes an open Runabout of unusual smartness and style.

The change from closed to open car can be made in two minutes, so that the Coupelet is quickly adaptable to all conditions of weather and driving.

It is especially popular with women who drive their own cars. As convenient and exclusive as an electric.

For physicians, architects, contractors, and all business and professional men who have to cover a great deal of territory it is admirably suited.

The Ford Coupelet may be driven twelve months in the year, in the city or over country roads, without personal discomfort, no matter what the weather.

Its distinctive style and attractiveness give it an exclusive appearance not found in any open runabout.

Buyers of this car will share in profits if we sell at retail 300,000 new Ford cars between August, 1914, and August, 1915.

Ford
THE UNIVERSAL CAR

It was called profit sharing!

In 1914 Ford announced a program that provided incentives to prospective purchasers. If, between August 1914 and August 1915, 300,000 new Fords were sold, then each buyer would share in the profits. It was a gimmick but it worked. Considerably more than 300,000 Fords were sold at a time when many manufacturers were going broke. Despite the fact that Henry Ford paid out millions, some of which came to Texas, the first ever auto rebate program was a huge success.

Henry Ford also pioneered another evolution in the automobile purchasing world, the installment plan.

Hot Tip Pal • More Smiles • Per Gal • Burma Shave

Now Easier Than Ever to Own a

Ford

Through the Ford Weekly Purchase Plan

$5 — will enroll you and start you on the way to ownership. We will put the money in a local bank—at interest. Each week make an additional payment. Soon your payments plus the interest paid by the bank will make the car yours.

So plan to get out into the fields and woods—down to the beach or stream—the family and you—in the Ford Sedan.

It is ready for pleasure or business anytime you step into the driver's seat and put your foot on the starter button—a car for all weather with real comfort for everyone. And now it is within your reach.

The Ford "Weekly Purchase Plan" was quite a deal — for Ford. Prospective buyers were encouraged to sign up to buy a car with only five dollars down. Ford put the money in an interest-bearing savings account for the buyer. Each week the buyer was urged to make additional deposits on the promise that "soon your payments plus interest paid by the bank will make the car yours." Since the price of a new Ford was $595 at the time, that meant that in about 2 years the car would be paid for. The theory, although it wasn't stated, was that people would become so anxious to get their car that they'd find a way to pay for it a little quicker than two years. And to think, from that beginning, we've come all the way to no money down and six years to pay. That's evolution.

In addition to creative financing, automobile manufacturers tried to lure customers to their products by offering optional equipment of every description. The options, always available at additional cost, were designed so buyers could customize their vehicles to their own liking. What customers did, however, was to begin to compete among themselves to see who could get the most on a car. And some took the practice to the extreme such as . . .

. . . Henry Moore of San Antonio. Shown here in a photo that appeared in the *San Antonio Light,* Henry is beside his 1923 Ford

which cost a whopping $1,900 or about twice what a regular model would have cost. What drove the price up were little extras like clocks, ash trays, special horns, bells, whistles, spotlights, several mirrors, and too much more to mention. It is just possible that Mr. Moore's Ford was the source of the phrase "all the bells and whistles."

The auto makers often competed among themselves to be the first to offer attractive options. Today, such wonderful devices as four-wheel brakes, windshield wipers and washers, heaters, spare tires, roll-down windows, door locks, gauges, and adjustable seats are usually standard equipment. All these devices, and many more, were originally high-priced options that could be added if you wanted them.

While the auto makers were scrambling to come up with new options, some enterprising Texas auto owners were coming up with options of their own.

Don't Pass Cars • On Curve Or Hill • If The Cops •
Don't Get You • The Morticians Will • Burma Shave

One Texan wanted to be comfortable when he tried to conduct business while driving in cold weather, so he installed a coal-burning stove behind the driver's seat. Fortunately, auto makers came up with a better way to heat the inside of cars.

Another man (below), perhaps tired of the price of gasoline, tried burning straight crude oil. He did away with the carburetor, vacuum tank, and muffler and attached a tank so the oil could flow to the engine. It was, perhaps, a nice try, but it never panned out and we're still stuck with gasoline.

Always Remember • On Any Trip • Keep Two Things • Within Your Grip • Your Steering Wheel • And • Burma Shave

Charles the Chauffeur

Charles, the chauffeur, and milady, Juliet,
The dashingest pair of the autoist set,
All primed for adventure, are out for a spiel,
On this fine country road, in their automobile.

As they dash down the pike, without quaver or hitch,
The farmers in front of them take to the ditch,
And the cohorts that follow are trailing afar
Like the Netherby clan after young Lochinvar.

After climbing a long grassy slope, at the top
The pulsing machine has been brought to a stop,
For the silt of the air, and microbic flies
Have reddened the lids of milady's bright eyes.

And Charles, at the signal, has stopped the machine,
And passed back the bottle containing Murine,
So milady leans back, and looks up at the sky
As the magic "two-drops" are dropped into each eye.

Now again they are off, at a forty mile pace,
With vision restored and new zest in the race;
And woe betide him who opposes their gait,
For he's booked for a serious tussle with fate.

The automobile, by some unwritten code,
Has won, in fee simple, all rights to the road;
And quite as true title indisputably, lies,
To the trite, but true saying, "Murine cures eyes."

**MURINE IS A TONIC FOR THE "AUTO EYE,"
SOOTHES AND QUICKLY CURES EYES
INFLAMED BY EXPOSURE TO STRONG WINDS AND DUST**

Some options were designed for the driver instead of the car. As evidenced by this vintage advertisement, a new product called Murine was great for curing "auto eye" caused by strong winds and blowing dust.

Some of the proposed safety devices never caught on with the public. One unsuccessful device was the 410-gauge automobile hijack-prevention shotgun pistol! The gun, specially designed to be carried on the front seat of a car so it could be grabbed quickly, fired either buckshot or slugs. The idea, according to the newspaper story at the time, was "If a highwayman slips up and tries to get rough, one discharge of buckshot would be sufficient to put a very abrupt end to his career."

It was advertised that, "When the public begins carrying the guns to any big extent, it is expected a very marked decrease will be noted in the number of holdups on country roads." The story concluded, "Some first-class advice is for all highwaymen to pick out their tombstones before going out in the future."

Despite some obvious advantages, the auto shotgun was never picked up by any auto manufacturer as standard equipment. Policemen everywhere are probably grateful that they weren't.

The general automobile public can also be glad the auto guns never caught on. If they had, the pistols might have been more than a deterrent. The special guns could have become an extension of an already potentially lethal product of automobile evolution which was the . . .

. . . woman driver.

The evolution of the automobile began about the same time that women decided there ought to be more to life than cooking food, washing clothes, cleaning house, and having babies. Women set out to prove they were equal to men, and what better place to accomplish that than behind the wheel of a car. It's been said that the Colt pistol made all men equal. Well, perhaps the automobile went a long way toward making men and women equal.

Unfortunately for the ladies, a lot of men believed that an automobile was intended for masculine use only. Those same men were certain that an automobile in the hands of a woman was nothing short of a weapon.

**A Girl · Should Hold On · To Her Youth · But Not ·
When He's Driving · Burma Shave**

And a very lethal weapon at that!

In all fairness, some ladies were, indeed, intimidated by the possibility of having to drive a car. For example, the lady driver above appears a little tense.

**Her Chariot · Raced 80 Per · They Hauled Away ·
What Had · Ben Hur · Burma Shave**

But she managed to flash a little . . . smile when she got the contraption stopped and was able to get out.

Men were not easily convinced that women belonged in the driver's seat and the male-dominated press usually went along.

This picture appeared in the *San Antonio Light* during the mid-1920s. The caption read " . . . shows woman's most serious mistake while driving an automobile — trying to drive and talk to back seat occupants at the same time." Please note, the car shown does not even have a back seat.

Life Is Sweet · But Oh How Bitter · To Love A
Gal · And Then · Not Git 'Er · Burma Shave

In another picture, also shown in the *Light*, a man tried to solve the problem of female drivers by installing a second steering wheel on the passenger side of the car. Wonder what happened if both drivers decided to turn — in opposite directions?

This photo supposedly prompted the lady not to let the man wrap his arm around her while driving. Instead, she was to put her arm around him. Now there's an idea that didn't work.

**If Huggin' • On Highways • Is Your Sport • Trade In
Your Car • For A Davenport • Burma Shave**

Of course, the female driver was not without her supporters. And none were stronger supporters of ladies behind the wheel than ...

Is Your Wife Marooned During the Day?

1921

Have you ever considered what is meant by the hundreds of cars parked in the business sections during working hours?

Most of them carried business men to work, leaving their wives and families at home, marooned because the family's one car is in daily use by the husband and father.

That is one reason why architects and builders now find that all suburban and many city homes must be provided with twin garages.

The Chevrolet Utility Coupé with Fisher Body makes an ideal extra car, especially in combination with a 5-passenger touring or sedan.

The wife finds it of every day utility for shopping, calling, taking the children to school in bad weather, etc.

Its price and upkeep are low yet the quality is high.

Chevrolet Motor Company
Division of General Motors Corporation

Detroit, Michigan

for Economical Transportation

Utility Coupé
$680
f. o. b. Flint, Mich.

Prices F. O. B. Flint, Mich.

Two Pass. Roadster	$510
Five Pass. Touring	525
Two Pass. Utility Coupé	680
Four Pass. Sedanette	850
Five Pass. Sedan	860
Light Delivery	510

There are now more than 10,000 Chevrolet Dealers and Service Stations Throughout the World.

Applications will be considered from high grade dealers in territory not adequately covered.

... the men who sold the cars.

**Heaven's Latest · Neophyte · Signaled Left ·
Then Turned Right · Burma Shave**

Almost from the very beginning, auto makers realized the potential of selling cars — lots of cars — to female drivers. In 1900 a women's magazine proclaimed, "It is not surprising that the automobile should be popular with women. Few women are experienced drivers, and as a rule they avoid the responsibility of managing a horse . . . The horseless carriage is more to their liking, inasmuch as they have only to learn how to handle a convenient lever to ride where they will, without any attendant whatever, and with perfect safety."

A 1910 advertisement on the Woods Electric automobile proclaimed "The chosen car of men of affairs, as well as the favorite conveyance of Her Highness, the American woman."

Also in 1910, Robert Ross wrote, "Let us make the surprising statement that woman not only can do but has done with the automobile everything of which man can boast — in some respects she has done it better . . . Almost any woman not an invalid can master its mysteries quite as well as a man, provided she has the will and patience to acquire the know-how. Certainly in the sphere of patience woman by nature is equipped to give man a long handicap. The woman motorist is not half so likely as a man is to swear and call loudly for a tow when anything goes wrong with the car. She will more probably set quietly to work to find the trouble and remedy it quite as thoroughly as if she were cleaning out the kitchen stove."

A 1924 Chandler advertisement was directed toward men, but women were the subject. "If you really want your wife to drive" was the question that began the ad. Assuming, perhaps incorrectly, that the answer was yes, the ad continued by urging the purchase of a Chandler so the ladies could "drive cooly through the thickest traffic . . . without the slightest worry."

By 1950 Packard was so intent on the female business that they changed their ad campaign from "Ask the man who owns one" to "Ask the woman who owns one." In 1955 Chrysler went after the ladies with its Dodge Custom Royal LaFemme model that came complete with matching rain cape, boots, umbrella, and purse.

Texas ladies were, quite naturally, right in step with their female counterparts around the nation. Unfortunately, lady drivers in Texas had two natural enemies.

**He Had The Ring • He Had The Flat • But She Felt His Chin
And That • Was That • Burma Shave**

One enemy was the hitchhiker who frequently turned out to be a hijacker unless, of course, he was running for governor of Texas.

The other enemy was the used car salesman. Sadly, ladies often proved an easy victim for unscrupulous used car peddlers out for a fast buck. Of course, not all used car salesmen pick on the ladies. Mr. Glenn Raines, Jr., pictured here, would never think of taking advantage of women. He prefers writers!

**Altho Insured • Remember, Kiddo • They Don't Pay You •
They Pay • Your Widow • Burma Shave**

Some women tried to strike back against their enemies. This lady hoped to discourage hitchhikers by traveling with a dummy man in the front seat. The prop may not not have talked much but he also didn't carry a gun!

Other women became astute automobile buyers in an effort to combat the dastardly used car salesman. Some were successful, others were not so lucky. When a lady ended up with a lemon, she often found a friend in the man . . .

. . . who ran the neighborhood filling station.

Big Mistake • Many Make • Rely On Horn •
Instead Of • Brake • Burma Shave

In the old days, before the price of gasoline made the phrase "full service" obsolete, there was always a crew standing by at the local filling station to help all motorists, male and female, with their driving requirements.

Just as the automobile evolved, so did the filling station. There was a time when you could get your gas while you watered the livestock.

Substitutes • Are Like A Girdle • They Find Some
Jobs • They Just • Can't Handle • Burma Shave

Eventually, stations became more sophisticated by adding options like indoor facilities for women. As for the men, well, have you ever heard the old saying: "Never eat anything that grows wild behind gas stations."

Eventually "filling stations" became service stations when the owners started offering repair services.

Grandpa Knows • It Ain't Too Late • He's Gone • To Git • Some Widder Bait • Burma Shave

Gas station evolution continued and they became a lot more sophisticated and . . .

. . . a whole lot bigger.

**This Will Never • Come To Pass • A Back-Seat •
Driver • Out Of Gas • Burma Shave**

Today, sooner or later everyone shows up at a gas station. With the current world oil situation, however, we can never be sure just how long everyone . . .

. . . will be welcome!

As auto evolution continued, more and more people began driving. That led to a new and very serious problem.

**Santa's · Whiskers · Need No Trimmin' · He Kisses
Kids · Not The Wimmin' · Burma Shave**

More and more cars meant fewer and fewer places to park.

When the streets filled up, parking stations (later to become parking lots) were invented, and although Texans squealed about fifteen cents a day to park, they paid.

**Passing Cars • When You Can't See • May Get
You • A Glimpse • Of Eternity • Burma Shave**

Someone, we'll never know who, had a bright idea to create covered parking, and in no time at all . . .

. . . we had multistory, fire-proof automobile storage facilities. Today, they're called parking garages.

**At A Quiz • Pa Ain't • No Whiz • But He Knows
How • To Keep Ma His • Burma Shave**

As for the few parking spots that still remain, some folks in Granbury offer some friendly instructions.

The people who run the Fort Worth convention center are pretty certain about where you better not park.

Of course, there are some who park where they want . . .

. . . no matter what the sign says.

Modern parking garages are often equipped with special gates and mechanical ticket-dispensing devices that have signs to tell you where to push for the ticket. One garage owner in Fort Worth, however, has a feeling for the language of Texas. His sign reads "Mash Here For Ticket!"

As more and more drivers appeared, the streets gradually became overcrowded, perhaps by people looking for parking places.

Eventually, the street became so crowded that something had to be done.

He Lit A Match • To Check Gas Tank • That's Why •
They Call Him • Skinless Frank • Burma Shave

63

Enter the human traffic signal. His job was to keep people from running into each other while dodging the cars himself.

Eventually, someone invented the automatic traffic light. The process was simple. First, cities simply put the lights on a pole in the middle of the street.

Romance Never Starts • From Scratch • Burma Shave

Second, they stationed a policeman on the curb to change the signals by remote control. The policeman above changed lights while listening to the Yankees in the 1925 World Series over a special radio headset. There is no record of how many accidents were caused every time Babe Ruth hit a home run.

Evolution continued when lights were strung from overhead wires. In the picture above, how do you suppose the car going through the intersection at the right managed to avoid being hit?

**You Can't Reach 80 • Hale And Hearty • By Driving 80 •
Home From • The Party • Burma Shave**

Perhaps because of continued traffic problems, evolution continued with the appearance of the human traffic light, version two. The officer wore battery-operated red lights on his chest and back and green lights on each arm. Theoretically, he could stand in the middle of the intersection and face the direction in which he wanted the traffic to stop. The idea didn't catch on and policemen everywhere cheered.

Another idea that never caught on was the special dog-equipped police motorcycle. Dogs everywhere cheered the decision to discontinue this particular service.

Police vehicles were very much a part of automobile evolution. The motorized police cruiser has continually . . .

. . . undergone change and improvement.

Week-old Beard • So Masked His Face • His Bulldog •
Chased Him • Off The Place • Burma Shave

Today, some law enforcement vehicles — especially the speedy Ford Mustangs — are more like rockets on wheels.

The driver of this particular unit allowed the picture to be taken while he was busy writing out a speeding ticket. Of course, I was totally innocent, but no amount of talking would convince the officer. During the interview, he asked my occupation. When told I was a writer, he naturally asked what I wrote. I said I wrote about Texas and that I was working on a new book entitled *Texas Highway Humor.*

"I sure hope you're gonna say something nice about the highway patrol," he said.

"I was," I replied, "until about ten minutes ago."

"You saw the radar," he said.

"Yea, but radar is not infallible," I countered.

"Well, sir," he said, "you can take that up with the judge."

"I intend to and I'm going to rethink saying anything nice about highway patrolmen." I added, with a smirk, "You may have the power of the radar but I have the power of the pen."

I was going to turn those guys every way but loose but I had a change of heart. It dawned on me that some lawmen might actually be able to read and they might just hold a grudge.

Just kidding, of course. Policemen deserve all the breaks they can get because the boys in blue are about all that stands between us and total anarchy. The "po-leece," as we say in Texas, have to deal with all sorts of problems from petty thieves to mass murderers. But one of the biggest problems facing the police, and all citizens as well, is a direct product of auto evolution. That problem is . . .

. . . the Drunk Driver

Whether he hits a telephone pole that "jumped out in front of him" or . . .

. . . went straight when he should have turned, the drunk driver is a real menace to himself and the automobiling public.

**Drinking Drivers • Nothing Worse • They Put •
The Quart • Before The Hearse • Burma Shave**

Of course, Texans have been drinking since before automobiles were invented. They have also been . . .

. . . drinking and driving since before automobiles were invented. Of course, a drunk farmer driving a horse-drawn wagon wasn't much of a threat, except to himself and perhaps the horses.

**Violets Are Blue • Roses Are Pink • On Grave
Of Those • Who Drive And Drink • Burma Shave**

When motorized vehicles came on the scene, drivers often filled their tank with fifty-cent-a-gallon gas at the local feed store and then filled themselves with five-cent-a-glass beer at the saloon next door.

Although it can't be proven, the first drive-in window in Texas may have been invented to secretly serve Budweiser to thirsty Texans.

**When Frisky • With Whiskey • Don't Drive •
'Cause It's • Risky • Burma Shave**

Naturally, the companies that made the liquor hoped to inspire purchases with catchy phrases like "Clear heads switch to Calvert." You have to wonder how long the heads stayed clear after people made the switch.

Those opposed to the evils of drink fought back with everything at their disposal. They tried parade floats which showed little children praying to be delivered from the evil of a father who drank the devil's own juice.

Car In The Ditch • Driver In Tree • Moon
Was Full • And So • Was He • Burma Shave

There were also anti-drink sign campaigns by law enforcement agencies.

With everyone using signs, the stage was set for a battle.

The One Who • Drives When • He's Been Drinking • Depends
On You • To Do His Thinking • Burma Shave

The battle of the . . .

If Every Sip • Fills You • With Zip • Then Your
Sipper • Needs A Zipper • Burma Shave

. . . billboards.

Unless prohibition comes back, the battle will continue. Of course, the whole problem could be avoided if drunks would . . .

... drive horses instead of cars!

For Painting • Cow-Shed • Barn Or Fence • That
Shaving Brush • Is Just Immense • Burma Shave

Despite the drunk drivers, the automobile evolution continued and there is no end in sight. In fact, the evolution continues at such a pace that some of the things invented because of automobiles are starting to disappear. How long . . .

. . . has it been since you and the entire gang hopped in the rumble seat and headed on down to the drive-in movie?

**Special Seats • Reserved In Hades • For Whiskered
Guys • Who Scratch • The Ladies • Burma Shave**

How long has it been since your burger was delivered by a car hop? And how long has it been since you had your milk delivered . . .

. . . right to — or even through — your door?

**A Chin · Where Barbed Wire · Bristles Stand · Is
Bound To Be · A No Ma'ams Land · Burma Shave**

Thanks to the automobile, mom and pop grocery stores have become convenience stores. Although 7-Eleven stores were the first convenience stores, they don't have a lock on great names for the little stores.

Others include: Wag-A-Bag; Come & Go; Whip In; Stop & Go; My T Quick; Short Stop; Fast Stop; Pit Stop; We B Quick; Stop & Shop; Cruz In; In & Out; and my personal favorite:

The proliferation of the automobile has probably been responsible for a dramatic increase in the number of restaurants in Texas. You can now eat . . .

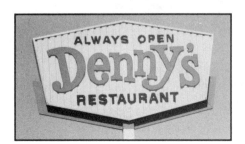

. . . at Denny's or at . . .

. . . Lenny's . . .

. . . but probably not at this sandwich shop.

You could try this restaurant but it isn't clear if Double Vision is just a name or what you get after eating there!

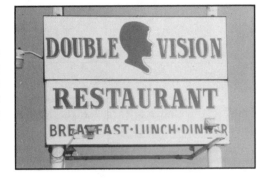

Train Wrecks Few • Reason Clear • Fireman
Never Hugs • Engineer • Burma Shave

Train Approaching • Whistle Squealing • Pause •
Avoid That • Rundown Feeling • Burma Shave

In San Antonio, you could try the Grill Sergeant or . . .

. . . the Texas version of the California Brown Derby. These restaurants specialize in German food. (If you believe that, I have some swamp land in Lubbock up for sale.)

Near Lake Tawakoni you could have some barbecue in probably the best named eatin' joint in Texas. Even if you don't buy anything, you're welcome to sit a spell and, you guessed it, shoot the bull.

**Drinking Drivers • Enhance Their • Chance • To
Highball Home • In An Ambulance • Burma Shave**

You can have lunch at this Texas cafeteria but don't wait around for Cannonball to come in.

If it's catfish you hanker, try this fast-food location in Midland but be sure to check the fish for hood ornaments.

If your tastes are more exotic, you might try the Big Texan in Amarillo. As for me, when it come to rattlesnakes, I prefer . . .

. . . the approach of this company in Midland.

One of the nice byproducts of automobile evolution is that there are many interesting things to see while you're out driving around looking for a place to eat. Here are a few of the sights you might encounter.

You could see the falls in Wichita Falls if you get there before they cut off the water at night. This is no joke. Seems the folks in Wichita Falls got tired of people asking where the waterfall was that inspired the town's name. Since the original dried up years ago, the town fathers built 'em a new one. And yes, they do occasionally turn off the water.

Pays Dividends · In Lady Friends · Burma Shave

Near Amarillo, you could see the famous Cadillac Ranch built by Stanley Marsh III so the people driving into town from New Mexico could have something to look at.

In downtown Midland, you can see the Statue of Liberty. Well, actually it's a replica and it's only about six feet tall, which is proof that things aren't always bigger in Texas.

Said Juliet · To Romeo · If You · Won't
Shave · Go Homeo · Burma Shave

On the other hand, you might see the world's biggest steer skull which is also in Midland.

Although most people are tying to do away with dangerous traffic circles, you can see a brand new one at this busy intersection in Plano.

If you survive the traffic circle in Plano, you might drive over to Rhome and buy fireworks from firemen. Talk about job security!

Some of the best sights in Texas are part of what I call the highway zoo. It includes a lot of bull in Amarillo, . . .

. . . dancing frogs at Carl's Corner, . . .

. . . steel elephants somewhere in North Central Texas, . . .

. . . a mule in Muleshoe (Note, you really can see a mule on any weekend except senior weekend when it is taken down because students in the past have taken liberties with the statue. Unfortunately, I arrived to take a picture of the mule on senior weekend. Although a clerk in a nearby convenience store volunteered to emulate the mule, I decided not to include her picture for fear she'd never live it down.),

. . . a rare jackalope in Fort Worth, and finally . . .

. . . cows in Abilene. As a public service to the thousands of motorists who have driven past these cows, they're not real, they're steel, which explains why they never seem to move.

Thanks to evolution, we now have big cars, little cars, fast cars, fancy cars, and cars that talk to you. They come from Japan, Germany, Italy, and even from Detroit. Some exotic models come with a television, a video game, and a microwave oven. One car maker even offers a special compartment to keep pizzas warm when you deliver 'em. Some cars come with on-board computers that do everything but drive for you and they're working on that. And a few Buicks now have a speedometer that projects your speed onto the windshield so you never have to take your eyes off the road.

As for the future, who knows? We may see plastic cars or even disposable cars. We may have vehicles that run on natural gas or even electricity, like they did when they were first invented. There may even be cars so advanced that computers and special tracking devices will allow the driver to take a nap while the car drives itself. We'll see.

There is, however, an ominous side to looking into a crystal ball to try to see the automobile future. With concerns over the environment mounting every day and millions of cars continuing to spit out carbon monoxide, is it possible that the automobile evolution will one day end in extinction of the species? Will the automobile perhaps yield to subways or trains or maybe even to giant pneumatic tubes? Who knows, the folks that created the "Star Trek" television series may have been ahead of their time, and one day we'll just say "Scotty, beam me to the mall" and, presto, we'll be there, if there are still such things as malls.

While the future may be clouded, one thing seems clear. It just doesn't look like horses are ever coming back. But . . .

. . . it they do there's a place in Amarillo waiting for them.

PART THREE

Signs of the Times

In Texas, signs come . . .

. . . in all sorts of sizes and designs.

Signs, in one form or another, have been around in Texas since long before automobiles. In the beginning, the signs were usually simple affairs and often were painted . . .

. . . directly onto the sides of buildings. Of course, no matter . . .

. . . how simple the sign, location was what counted.

It's Best For • One Who Hits • The Bottle • To Let
Another • Use The Throttle • Burma Shave

In Texas, there were some locations that had it all!

For a couple of generations, the Flying Red Horse sign atop the old Mobil Building in Dallas had a great location. Today, you can hardly see the sign because of all the taller buildings.

**He's The Boy · The Gals Forgot · His Line
Was Smooth · His Chin Was Not · Burma Shave**

92

If you spend any time at all driving in Texas, you'll see lots of signs — all kinds and types of signs. The ones that follow are some of my favorites.

Spelling, is of course critical in signs. In Texas, TIRS should have been TARS . . .

. . . and DRINKIN' certainly should have been DRANKIN.'

This man definitely needs to know the difference between two and too. There is no record on whether or not he found a twenty-two-year-old wife willing to keep him and his house clean.

Unless Your Face • Is Stinger Free • You
Better Let • Your Honey Be • Burma Shave

The person who put up this sign must have been from the North because he was clueless on how to spell "you all."

The correct spelling is shown in this sign in front of a chapel near Wichita Falls. Using horseshoes for "Cs" was a nice Texas touch.

This is one of the most famous signs in Texas, but how do you spell don't?

Either this sign should have been bigger or they should have used smaller letters.

Each year, thousands of tourists travel Interstate 35 south through Waco. Undoubtedly, most of those tourists have wondered who in the heck is Mother Neff. As a public service to those travelers, Mrs. Neff was the mother of former Texas governor Pat Neff. The park was named in her honor because she donated two and a half acres of land for the creation of the very first state park in Texas. Now you'll know in case that question ever comes up in a trivia contest.

Many of those same travelers might have also wondered about this sign. Well, H.O.T. stands for Heart Of Texas where, in the summer, it is often very HOT.

And one final public service announcement. Judging from this sign, it appears the folks in Waco have run out of good names for new roads. If you think of any names, why not send 'em to the mayor of Waco. I'm sure he'd appreciate it!

Some signs are very simple and yet they leave you wondering. "What exactly is a Roach Unit anyway?"

In this case, you have to wonder how much extra it would be for some pizza.

If you drive by this sign, you have to wonder two things. "First, what kind of door wouldn't fail and second, are they expecting an explosion?"

Who could possibly come upon this sign in Central Texas and not ponder the perplexing question, "Is there only one rock that can fall?"

Hardly anyone can pass a sign like this without wondering "How do they do that?"

If you saw this sign in Midland, you're bound to wonder "What if this isn't the place?"

I'd be willing to bet a lot of people passed this sign and asked themselves, "Do I know what a haute couture is?" Do you?

Some signs actually make sense. Considering the type of car many DPS officers drive (see page 68), it's appropriate that their offices are on Missile Road!

If you ever get stopped by one of those officers and feel like telling him to go to ... well, be subtle about it and just invite him to go west of Interstate 35 on Highway 306 and follow the signs!

Speaking of law enforcement, this unusual sign is in front of an alley frequently used by Dallas police officers. If such a sign is effective, it makes you wonder why you never see them in front of alleys you and I frequent. On the other hand, perhaps we're not supposed to frequent alleys!

98

With so many signs around, there are occasional battles. A Diamond Shamrock in San Marcos offered a free car wash with purchase. The Exxon station across the street had no car wash so they offered the next best thing, a free vacuum with purchase.

Near Lake Whitney, a honkytonk called the Cottage Club was once closed and the owners explained why with a sign out front.

The folks next door lost no time in putting up a sign explaining why they were open. In case you haven't guessed . . .

. . . the establishment next door was a church!

The fact is, churches are often a good source for some creative signs. Perhaps the most famous was the sign that was once outside a Dallas church. It read:

LAST CHANCE TO PRAY BEFORE ENTERING FREEWAY

Some other Texas church classics are:

LIVING IS LIKE LICKING HONEY OFF A THORN
BE HUMBLE OR YOU STUMBLE
THE WAGES OF SIN NEVER GO UNPAID
A GOOD WORD IS AS EASILY SAID AS A BAD ONE
THE FISH AREN'T BITING
SO WHY NOT COME TO CHURCH

And my personal favorite:

Now there was a sermon I wish I'd heard.

100

Signs with business names offer some real fun on occasion. In Houston there's a used clothing store called Wear It Again, Sam; Dallas has its One Main Place and there's a beauty salon in North Texas called One Mane Place; then there's the popular barber shop called Hair Force One; and who could forget the Best Little Warehouse in Texas. Here are some other clever ones:

Perhaps my favorite name is on a tavern near the north end of Fort Hood in Central Texas. The name is simple and yet it says so much. The tavern is called . . .

. . . He Ain't Here. It's probably more than a name; it's a philosophy.

Strip centers offer wonderful possibilities for signs. Anyone with kids will appreciate the Sweat Shop being located next door to Planned Parenthood.

What about this funeral home in Plano? If you fell over dead when your income tax was prepared, you wouldn't have far to go. That's service!

Some signs are worth paying attention to. When the picture above was taken I could hear the distinct sound of machine gun fire in the distance. I was more than happy to honor the "keep out" part.

These signs take on added importance when you consider they're usually on the back of very large trailers.

You may have seen many of these signs without paying much attention, right? But if you see one . . .

. . . on the front of a truck, it makes you stop and wonder, "Just exactly how many lessons has the driver had?"

You might have seen a thousand signs offering vehicle protection devices and not paid any attention. But if you saw this sign, it might give you a reason to consider an alarm.

**When You Drive • If Caution Ceases • You
Are Apt • To Rest • In Pieces • Burma Shave**

No one uses more signs in the Lone Star State than the state itself. Official signs are everywhere! And most seem to make perfect sense.

Spring Has Sprung • The Grass Has Riz • Where Last Year's • Careless Driver Is • Burma Shave

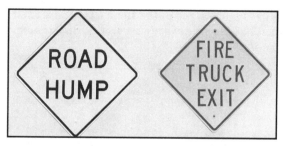

Some state signs, however, are a little confusing. Such questions as, "What *is* a road hump?" and "Can *only* fire trucks exit? sometimes arise. Other questions that you may one day ask yourself are . . .

"What exactly does *travel at own risk* mean?"

"*Whose* sight is limited?" or "Why do I need to know about damaged guard rails anyway? Am I gonna fall off?"

**Proper Distance • To Him Was Bunk • They Pulled
Him Out • Of Some Guy's Trunk • Burma Shave**

All Texans have a right to be proud of their highways. Anyone who doubts that ought to make a trip to Oklahoma. The Texas Highway Department has done a great job, but it's hard not to question the validity of spending tax dollars on some signs.

For instance, why does the state of Texas think we need to check our speedometers? Do they know something we don't? And isn't the first rule of driving to keep your eyes on the road? How do you do that while trying to watch for signs and check the exact mileage on your speedometer at the same time?

And speaking of mileage, what about these signs that appear literally all over the state. What do they mean and why are they necessary? More importantly, how many tax dollars were required to put up the signs? We'll never know.

At first glance, some signs appear to be useful.

The Wolf • Is Shaved • So Neat And Trim • Red Riding Hood • Is Chasing Him • Burma Shave

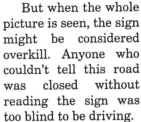

But when the whole picture is seen, the sign might be considered overkill. Anyone who couldn't tell this road was closed without reading the sign was too blind to be driving.

The health department probably spent a lot of tax dollars putting these little signs up all over the state. Wouldn't it have made more sense, and saved a lot of money, to only put up signs where the water supply was *not* approved?

There are places where deer crossing signs are needed, but whose job is it to tell the deer they can only cross for the next 22 miles?

Cattle Crossing • Means Go Slow • That Old
Bull • Is Some • Cow's Beau • Burma Shave

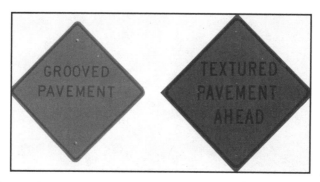

Grooved pavement signs are perhaps necessary to warn drivers of what to expect, but what in the world is *textured* pavement? Is that anything like designer pavement?

Other signs seem curiously incomplete. If livestock are roaming free, shouldn't there be a "slow down," "caution," or "go the other way" message on the sign? Better yet, instead of putting up signs, why not make the ranchers keep their cows in a pasture where they belong?

Some signs are, of course, necessary.

Is He Lonesome • Or Just Blind • The Guy
Who Drives • So Close Behind • Burma Shave

But is it necessary to have two signs only six feet apart?

A few signs just naturally arouse curiosity. For instance, exactly when will the *temporary* end, and what speed limit is hidden by the tape and who put on the tape?

There are occasions when tax dollars pay for more than just highway signs. For example, these signs often appear in roadside parks along interstate highways. And what does the arrow point to?

Bewiskered · Kisses · Defrost · The Misses · Burma Shave

What else? It is interesting to note that the fake fire hydrants, paid for by tax dollars, are located just a few feet away from bushes provided by nature. Where dogs are concerned, don't bushes usually serve the same purpose as fire hydrants? Just wondering, that's all.

Of course, Texas has hundreds of other signs. There are so many, in fact, that no one can possibly see or even obey them all. With that in mind, here's my idea of the ten most ignored signs in Texas.

No 10. Admit it now, how many times have you seen these speed zone signs and automatically slowed down? Me either.

No. 9. You've surely seen a number of these signs in Texas, right? And generally you also see that they are being . . .

The Wolf • Who Longs • To Roam And Prowl • Should
Shave Before • He Starts to Howl • Burma Shave

... almost totally ignored!

No. 7. So what if it's state law, no one ever pays attention to these signs.

No. 8. These signs are usually ignored, probably because you often see them in August when it's 103 degrees in the shade and you know there isn't ice on the bridge.

No 6. The double white lines are almost always in high traffic areas and are usually ignored unless the law is around.

To Kiss • A Mug • That's Like A Cactus • Takes More
Nerve • Than It Does Practice • Burma Shave

No 5. The number 1 most ignored sign by drunk drivers. Some drivers have made rolling a stop sign an art. Susie Seltzer of Midland swears she thought these signs meant Slightly Tap On Pedal.

No. 4. The way drivers on freeway access roads ignore these signs you'd think the suckers were printed with invisible ink.

No 3. This would have been a runaway No 1 if the powers that be hadn't come to their senses and raised the limit to 65.

No 2. How many times have you been going 65 and a truck passed you like you were standing still? Wonder why those guys never get speeding tickets?

And finally, the No 1 most ignored sign in Texas is . . .

Can someone — anyone — explain why so many drivers get in the left lane (the fast lane) and then go so slow you think they are homesteading?

Honorable mention in the most ignored signs list is the now famous ...

Don't mess with Texas.

The state of Texas is a big place with miles and miles of miles and miles. If all motorists deposited their trash along the highway, we'd be in a world of garbage.

The state tries to control litter bugs with special signs and ...

. . . special incentives *not* to litter. In case you've ever wondered what the difference is between a $10 fine and a $1,000 fine, the answer, according to several judges, is your *attitude*. Yes sir, any time you get caught littering you could, if you sass the judge, get clipped for a grand. Think about that the next time you throw out a gum wrapper.

In addition to the state, some cities are equally interested in your not littering!

As you travel the state, you'll notice that many cities and towns offer some sign levity for your enjoyment. As you may know, the Dallas - Fort Worth area is known as the Metroplex. Well, out in far West Texas they have a "plex" of their own.

The Hero · Was Brave And Strong · And Willin' · She Felt His Chin · Then Wed The Villain · Burma Shave

It's the Greater Mule-Plex, a.k.a. Muleshoe.

If you can find Rhonesboro and if you can pass a test, you might receive a degree. It's a BS in Possumology. No kidding.

Some people claim Davy Crockett himself named this town.

I always thought the grand canyon of Texas was in Canyon not in Amarillo.

You may have heard that Fort Worth claims to be where the West begins. Well Sweetwater claims to be where the . . .

... best begins!

As you travel Texas, you cannot help but notice that there are some exotic destinations.

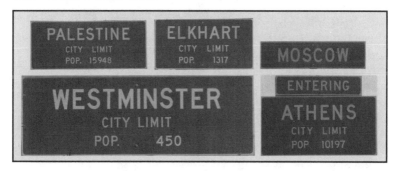

Some of the more famous Texas destinations are: BOSTON, WARSAW, TAMPICO, DUBLIN, TURKEY, HOLLAND, SCOTLAND, INDIA, DETROIT, EGYPT, JERICO, LIVERPOOL, LONDON, ITALY, IRELAND, TRINIDAD, TOKIO, TROY, VIENNA, TUNIS, STOCKHOLM and, naturally, UTOPIA and PARADISE, TEXAS.

And what's the best exotic destination in Texas? My personal favorite is . . .

. . . Beverly
Hills, Texas.

Some Texas towns are so friendly, they take the time to invite you back. As a public service to the folks in Buda, you should know that the town's name is pronounced Bew-da and not Boo-da. When said correctly, the phrase "Keep it Bew-da-ful" sounds a lot better.

As you travel Texas, you'll cross a lot of creeks, and some of them have interesting names like . . .

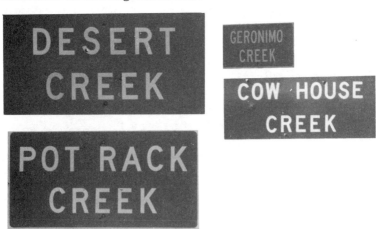

Occasionally, you cross a creek and have to wonder . . .

WOMAN HOLLERING CREEK

. . . how in the world did it get its name?

When you're not crossing creeks, other things may be crossing the road in front of you. Fortunately, there are usually plenty of signs to warn you what to expect. Some signs . . .

. . . are fairly routine and others are . . .

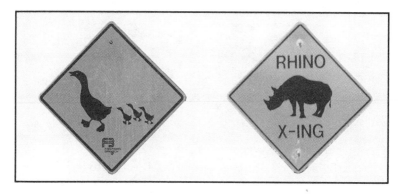

. . . even cute.

A Guy • Who Drives • A Car Wide Open • Is Not Thinkin' • He's Just Hopin' • Burma Shave

Then there are a couple that should make you perk right up and take notice! Ever seen a pickup run over by a twenty-ton tank? Me either and I don't want to, especially if I'm driving.

If I was involved in a collision with a tank, I believe I'd want my seat belt securely fastened, which is appropriate since wearing seat belts when driving is a state law in Texas.

Compliance with the law is urged with billboards and . . .

. . . smaller signs, although the city of Fort Worth is a bit more creative with its signs. Makes you wonder if the person who designed these signs might have gone to school in Austin.

**The Boy Who Gets • His Girl's Applause • Must Act •
Not Look • Like Santa Claus • Burma Shave**

One category of sign that has been around a long time are . . .

. . . billboards.

Most people don't know it but billboards were almost outlawed before they became so numerous. When the automobile first became popular, advertisers quickly realized the value of erecting signs along the roads promoting their products and services. It seemed that as more people started driving, more and more billboards sprang up, a fact that did not escape the notice of many people who didn't particularly care for the unsightly signs.

A grass roots uprising was organized to try to prevent the signs from continuing to multiply. The protesters claimed, perhaps rightfully so, that if billboard companies were not kept in check, they would eventually erect so many signs that the scenic beauty of the countryside would be forever ruined. Anyone who has ever traveled the roads of Texas knows that the protesters were correct. Some of the best views in the state are almost ruined because some joker stuck up a billboard to advertise something or other.

The billboard companies countered with some freedom of speech (and advertising) arguments and the battle raged on. Eventually the courts and even the U.S. Congress became involved. In the end, the protesters met with only partial success. There are some limits controlling the use of billboards, but for the most part, outdoor advertising companies are free to do their thing.

Other than protesters, the billboard companies also found out they had some natural enemies.

**Don't • Try Passing • On A Slope • Unless You
Have • A Periscope • Burma Shave**

One billboard enemy was wind and . . .

. . . the other was water. The photographer who snapped this shot found humor in the fact that a billboard advertising Canada Dry was almost under water.

If You Have • A Double Chin • You've Two • Good
Reasons • To Begin Using • Burma Shave

This photograph, courtesy of Bill Miller, Jr., shows a pair of billboards that were almost drowned. Notice that one shows a canoe and the other is a recruiting poster for the Navy!

Since it appears we are stuck with billboards, one thing we can find some comfort in is the fact that many of the signs are very creative. A lot of people have spent a lot of hours coming up with catchy phrases and interesting signs designed to catch our eye. Possibly the most creative billboard company in Texas . . .

. . . is Bob Miller, Jr.'s Duplex Advertising company in Temple, Texas. Bob has been involved with outdoor advertising for many years, and some of the creations from his companies have become legends.

Bob led the fight to have Temple officially named the wildflower capital of Texas. Rumor has it that Bob now spends all his spare time planting wildflowers to prove his point.

**Doesn't Kiss You • Like She Useter? • Perhaps She's
Seen • A Smoother Rooster! • Burma Shave**

Bob also proclaimed Temple to be the center of the universe! Other Miller classics include . . .

. . . a public service to Texas Aggies and . . .

. . . a variation of the "Buy American" theme.

She Eyed • His Beard • And Said No Dice • The Wedding's Off • I'll *COOK* The Rice • Burma Shave

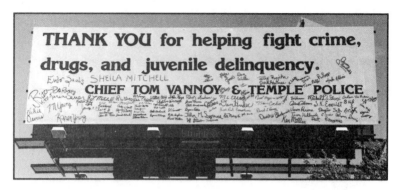

Bob showed his civic pride by thanking the Temple police.

He showed his pride in Texas with this award winner.

And although Bob didn't design it, Duplex did put up my personal favorite billboard of all time.

Bristly Beard · Or Silky Fuzz · Just Shave 'Em
Back · To Where · They Was · Burma Shave

Sometimes Bob runs into problems. In this case he told the crew to paint the sign and they did.

In this case some seniors took it upon themselves to change the sign and it was several days before anyone noticed.

Although this sign seems normal enough, when it was first installed it was on land in front of a popular bordello. The sign was quickly removed in an effort to keep the jokes from spreading.

Of course, there are lots of sign companies and lots of great billboards throughout Texas. The following are some of the best.

Wonder what they sell at a Country *Mouse* Store?

The Nike Factory Store in Hillsboro had some fun with this sign. They also have another one which simply says, "Meet Bo," referring to their commercials by Bo Jackson. Again, they were just kidding, but the sign does raise an important question. Since Bo Jackson has been injured and his career is in jeopardy, does that mean he might lose his shoe contract? And if he does, will he then be known as Shoeless Bo Jackson?

Don't Stick • Your Elbow • Out So Far • It Might Go
Home • In Another Car • Burma Shave

This billboard, in Crockett, Texas, marks the spot where Davy Crockett stopped to drink from a spring on his way to the Alamo. Today, you can drink from that same spring thanks to a water fountain that was installed some time after Davy left.

And I always thought it was the Mockingbird!

If you get one of these, . . .

Who ya' gonna call?

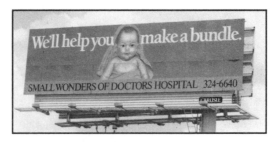

They help you make a bundle so you can then spend a bundle raising it.

On the other hand, maybe babies are worth a bundle.

Don't you wish savings and loans would pass some back!

Maybe this is why so many banks have gone under!

This billboard could also be used for the Miss Texas pageant.

Mark your calender — see ya there!

Only if I ante up.

What if you've given all you have and you're nowhere near having it all?

A take-off on an old song.

A take-off on a popular bumper sticker.

A clever play on words that sounds worth a try.

Sound advice.

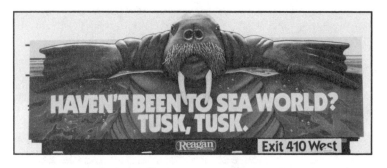

Some of the best billboards are those that appear in a series. Here's a good example:

And the last one (drum roll, please) was . . .

And that, my friends, brings us to a . . .

I'd like to leave you with some good advice . . .

. . . and my favorite Burma Shave sign:

**If Crusoe'd · Kept His Chin · More Tidy · He Might
Have Found · A Lady Friday · Burma Shave**